USBORNE

CHILDREN'S PICTURE ATLAS

Illustrated by Linda Edwards

Written by Ruth Brocklehurst
Designed by Doriana Berkovic

Cartographer: Craig Asquith

Consultants:
Prof. Rex Walford
Dr. Margaret Rostron
Prof. Michael Hitchcock

Contents

The Universe

We live in a Universe that's so enormous it's almost impossible to imagine. To picture it, you need to start small, then think big.

A town has streets with houses, shops, schools and other buildings.

Towns and cities

People live in all kinds of places around the world. Most people live in houses or apartments in towns. Really big towns are called cities.

Countries

The land around the world is divided into different countries. Countries usually have towns, cities, farmland and wild countryside.

This small country has towns, fields, mountains and sandy beaches. Not all countries are islands like this one.

Planet Earth

A country is just a small part of the land on the planet Earth. The Earth is a huge ball of rock floating in space. Land covers part of it and the rest is sea.

The Sun is a star. It gives out light and heat.

Mercury

Earth

Venus

Jupiter

Mars

Uranus

Neptune

Pluto

Saturn

This picture shows all the planets in the Solar System, and Pluto, which scientists now call a dwarf planet.

The Solar System

The Earth is one of eight planets that go around the Sun. Together, the Sun and these planets are called the Solar System. The Earth is the only planet where people, plants and animals live.

The Universe

There are trillions of stars shining in space and the Sun is one of them. A large group of stars is called a galaxy. The Sun belongs to a galaxy called the Milky Way. All the galaxies in space make up the Universe.

On a clear night, you can see thousands of stars.

What are maps?

Maps are pictures that show places as they look from above. They usually make places look much smaller than they really are. A book, like this one, full of maps is called an atlas.

Spacecraft called satellites are used to take photographs of the Earth from space.

This is a satellite photograph. It shows part of London.

Making maps

Mapmakers often use photographs of places taken from above to help them draw maps. They also measure the ground to find out the sizes of places and how far they are from each other.

What maps show

When mapmakers draw maps, they just include the important details. Maps often have shading, labels and little pictures to tell you more about a place.

This is a picture map of the same place as the photograph above.

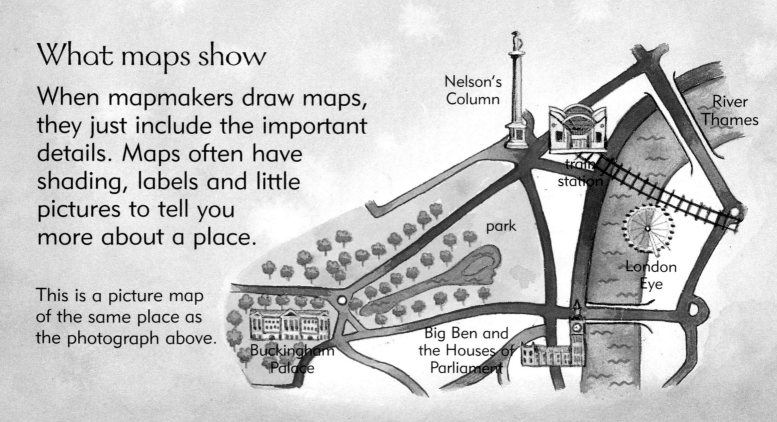

Nelson's Column

River Thames

train station

park

London Eye

Buckingham Palace

Big Ben and the Houses of Parliament

The round Earth

Because the Earth is a ball shape, a photograph can only show one side of it. Mapmakers can show the whole Earth, as it actually looks, by making a model of it. A model Earth is called a globe.

This satellite photograph shows one side of the Earth from space.

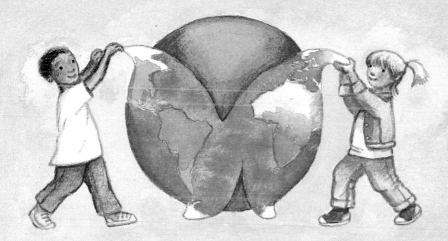

If the surface of a globe could be peeled off, this is how it would look.

Peeled Earth

To make a flat map of the round Earth, mapmakers draw the Earth as though its curved surface has been peeled off and opened out flat.

Filling the gaps

The peeled map isn't much use because it has lots of gaps. Some parts have to be squashed or stretched to make a map without gaps.

This is a peeled map. You can see a world map without gaps on pages 28–29.

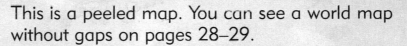
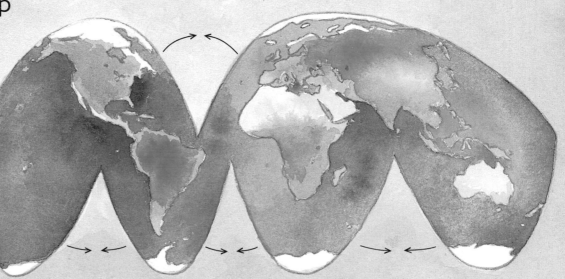

7

Countries and cities

There are more than 190 countries in the world. The place where one country meets another is called a border. On the maps in this book, the borders are shown as red dotted lines.

Borders

Many country borders are along rivers or mountains. Sometimes, borders are marked by fences or walls.

Some borders have gates where guards check who goes in and out.

Papua New Guinea has more than 700 islands like this.

Island groups

Some countries, such as Papua New Guinea, are made up of lots of islands. The maps in this book show their borders in the sea around the islands.

Can you find these things on the maps?

Big Ben

Parthenon

St. Basil's Cathedral

Forbidden City

Eiffel Tower

Big cities

Skyscrapers can fit many hundreds of people into a small space.

Big cities can be very crowded. Many people work or live in tall buildings called skyscrapers. The black circles ● on the maps show where the biggest cities are.

This is the White House, in Washington DC, USA. The President of the USA lives and works here.

Country capitals

The people in charge of a country work in a city called the capital. Lots of capitals have big, grand buildings. Capital cities are shown as black squares ■.

Street parties

In some cities, there are street parties called carnivals. People dress up and dance in the streets.

At carnivals, people wear bright, fancy costumes.

Blue Mosque

Winter Palace in St. Petersburg

Leaning Tower of Pisa

Sydney Opera House

Statue of Liberty

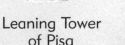

People

Millions and millions of people live around the world. In different parts of the world, people may look, talk and behave differently.

Japanese children wear kimonos for festivals and special occasions.

Dressing up

In some places, people dress up for special occasions in a style of clothes that people wore long ago. The clothes they wear are called traditional costumes.

Religions

A religion is a way of thinking about the world. Some people believe in one God and others believe in many gods. Most religions have holy places or buildings where people go to pray or think.

In Jerusalem, in Israel, there are many places where Christians, Muslims and Jewish people go to pray.

Can you find these people on the maps?

Guarani people   Zulu dancer   sitar player   rugby player   highland piper

Music and dancing

Many countries have their own styles of music and dancing. Some places have their own traditional musical instruments too.

Flamenco is a Spanish style of dancing to guitar music.

Chinese people often eat using chopsticks.

Eating

People around the world eat all kinds of foods. They also have many ways of cooking and eating. Food is transported long distances, so people can taste dishes from all around the world.

Sharing interests

Although people can be very different, they also have lots in common. With travel, television, telephones and the Internet, it's easy for people to share ideas.

People from all around the world get together to play soccer.

conga drummer

Tibetan monks

Hopi dancer

girl in a poncho

American football player

11

Getting around

There are many ways to get from one place to another. Journeys can be made by air, land or water. Some are quicker than others.

Jumbo jet planes can carry more than 600 people.

This Japanese bullet train's shape helps it go faster.

Long distances

Planes and trains can carry lots of people at a time. They make long journeys, at great speeds, all around the world.

River rides

It is difficult to build roads in thick forests. The easiest way to travel there is along a river.

Many people canoe along the Amazon River.

Can you find these things on the maps?

basket boat

desert truck

traditional junk (boat)

Trans-Siberian Express

helicopter

Pedal power

In the busy city streets of India and China, many people use bicycles and rickshaws, instead of cars.

Rickshaws are pulled by people on foot or on bicycles. They are small, so they don't get stuck in traffic jams.

Children can ride on the back of a snowmobile.

Icy journeys

In snowy places, people use snowmobiles and sleds to get around. Snowmobiles have skis, instead of wheels, so they glide easily over the snow.

Watery city

A canal is a man-made river. In Venice, in Italy, there are canals instead of roads. People there use boats to get around the city.

Many people in Venice ride in boats called gondolas. They use poles to push the gondolas along.

Ice and snow

☐ The white parts of the maps show places that are covered with ice and snow. The coldest places in the world are the Arctic in the north and Antarctica in the south.

The poles

The most northern place on Earth is called the North Pole. Whichever way you go from there is south. The South Pole is on the other side of the world.

Arctic terns spend half the year in the Arctic and the other half in Antarctica.

Penguins huddle together to keep out the cold.

Poles apart

Penguins and polar bears never meet in the wild. This is because penguins live in Antarctica and polar bears only live in the Arctic.

Polar bears have thick fur to keep them warm.

Can you find these things on the maps?

ice fish

humpback whale

American science station

Arctic fox

Saami people

Keeping warm

People in frozen lands need to wrap up warm outside. Inuit people, who live in the Arctic, wear thick coats called parkas to keep out the cold.

These Inuit children are dressed in traditional parkas.

Science in the snow

Antarctica is a large, cold island. There, scientists from all over the world work in science stations. They go there to study the weather and to find out about the animals that live there.

Scientists can measure how cold it is in the sky by fixing a thermometer to a weather balloon.

Icebreaker ships are strong and heavy. They break up the frozen ocean, clearing a way for other ships.

Frozen sea

There isn't any land at the North Pole, but much of the sea is frozen solid all year. In the summer, some of the ice melts and breaks up into huge chunks called icebergs.

Deserts

The yellow parts of the maps show the deserts. Deserts are dry places which are sandy or rocky. They are very hot during the day and cold at night.

Flamingos flying over the Atacama Desert.

In sandy deserts, wind blows the sand into hills called dunes.

Desert records

The Sahara, in Africa, is the biggest, hottest desert in the world. The driest desert is the Atacama, in Chile. In parts, it hasn't rained for 400 years.

Oasis

An oasis is a place in the desert where there is water. Plants grow there and animals and people go there to drink.

These people are collecting water from an oasis.

Can you find these animals on the maps?

fennec fox

jerboa

blue-tongued skink

scorpion

rattlesnake

Thirsty animals

Camels can drink lots of water at once, then go for a week without any. They are suited to life in the desert in other ways too.

Camels can close their nostrils to stop sand from blowing in.

They have wide feet so they don't sink into the sand.

Plant survival

Desert plants have different ways of surviving in such dry places.

Many desert flowers only burst into bloom just after it rains.

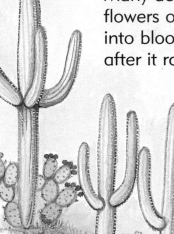

Cactus plants store water in their stems.

Desert people

Many desert people don't live in one place. They move around with their animals, to find water and food.

Bedouins are desert people. Some of them live in camps like this.

17

Grasslands

Grasslands are flat, open spaces where lots of grasses grow. They are shaded in pale green on the maps. Different types of grasses grow in different places around the world.

Safaris

The grassland in Africa is called the savanna. In the hot, dry season, the grass is dry and golden. People go on tours called safaris to see the wild animals that live there.

Lions spend most of their time resting.

A group of zebras is called a herd.

Eating grass

Many savanna animals, such as zebras and antelopes, are grass-eaters. They live in large groups so they are safer from hunters, such as lions.

Can you find these animals on the maps?

kangaroos

guanaco

buffalo

giraffe

meerkats

Green, green grass

In Northern Europe and New Zealand, the weather is often cool and rainy. The grass there is lush and green and good for cows and sheep to eat.

Farmers get wool and meat from sheep.

Cowboys called gauchos round up cows on horseback.

The pampas

The grassland in South America is called the pampas. Farmers there keep thousands of cows on farms called ranches. Cows are kept for meat and milk.

Combine harvesters are huge machines that cut wheat and other crops.

Grassland farming

Most of the world's wheat and corn grows on the grasslands in Russia and North America. Farmers there use big machines to collect the grain.

lion

giant anteater

African elephant

oryx

rhea

19

Forests

The dark green parts of the maps show where forests are. Different types of forests grow in different parts of the world.

Conifer trees

Coniferous forests grow in cold places, with snowy winters. Conifer trees have long, thin leaves, called needles. They stay green all year round.

Conifer trees grow seed cones that squirrels eat.

Tropical rainforests

More kinds of plants live in rainforests than anywhere else.

Rainforests grow in parts of the world where it is hot and rainy all the time. They are steamy places with towering trees, thick bushes and millions of animals.

Can you find these things on the maps?

blue morpho butterfly

armadillo

red fox

raccoon

anaconda

20

Trees in winter

In places with mild weather, many trees lose their leaves in the winter. The leaves turn red and golden before they fall.

The winter wind blows dead leaves from the trees.

In the spring, fresh green leaves grow.

How old is a tree?

You can find out the age of a tree by counting the number of rings in its trunk. A tree has a ring for each year of its life.

When a tree is cut down, you can see the rings in its trunk.

Giant pandas only eat bamboo.

Forests of bamboo

Giant pandas live in bamboo forests, in the mountains of China. There, the bamboo grows tall and thick. Only around 600 giant pandas live in the wild.

grizzly bear

wild mushrooms

lumberjack
(forester)

chimpanzee

toucan

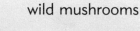

Mountains

Mountains are high, rocky places. Their highest points are called peaks. Tiny mountain shapes on the maps show where the biggest mountains are.

Ski lifts take skiers up and down mountains.

Snowy peaks

The higher up a mountain you go, the colder and windier it gets. On the high slopes, it is too cold for trees to grow. The highest peaks are so cold that they are covered with snow, even in the summer.

Snow leopards have pale fur, to blend in with their snowy surroundings.

Climbing creatures

Many mountain animals, such as goats and snow leopards, are excellent climbers. They also have extra-thick fur to keep out the chilly winds.

Mighty mountains

A line of mountains is called a range. The Andes, in South America, is the longest mountain range in the world.

Some farmers in the Andes keep llamas for their wool.

Climbers use ropes and hooks to help them cling onto rocky ledges upside down.

Climbing

Mount Everest is the highest mountain in the world. Many adventurers travel to Asia to make the difficult climb to its highest peak.

Mountain birds

Some birds, such as eagles and condors, live high up in mountains. They build their nests on rocky cliffs and narrow ledges.

Condors lay their eggs where other animals can't reach them.

Can you find these things on the maps?

bald eagle

Mount Everest

yak

chamois

Ural owl

23

Rivers and lakes

These people are using reed boats to cross Lake Titicaca.

The dark blue lines and shading on the maps show where rivers and lakes are. The water in them comes from rain and melted snow. Many towns are built near rivers and lakes and lots of animals live in and near them.

A mountain lake

The highest lake in the world is Lake Titicaca, in South America. People there make boats from reeds that grow around the lake.

A river's journey

Rivers start high up in mountains, and flow downhill into lakes or the sea. The water slowly wears away the rock to make a dip in the ground, called a valley.

The Colorado River, in the USA, flows through the world's deepest valley. It is called the Grand Canyon.

A holy river

For many people, the Ganges River, in India, is a holy place. People from around the world go there to bathe in its water.

The water in a waterfall flows fast, and looks white and frothy.

People bathe in the Ganges River during religious festivals.

A waterfall

When a river flows over a steep step in the land, the water tumbles down it and makes a waterfall.

Muddy mouths

The wide, muddy place where a river joins the sea is called the river mouth. Lots of birds live there because the mud is full of plants and tiny fish to eat.

Crocodiles and herons live by the river mouth of the Nile, in Egypt.

Can you spot these things on the maps?

capybara

piranha

Caspian seal

hippopotamus

felucca boat

Seas and oceans

More than half of the Earth is covered with the salty water of seas and oceans. There are five large oceans and lots of smaller seas. They are shown in blue on the maps.

A large group of fish is called a school.

Sea life

Different types of animals and plants live in different parts of the sea. Giant squid live deep under the sea, but crabs and shrimps live in shallow water, near the shore.

Blue whales are the world's biggest animals. An adult blue whale weighs about the same as 20 elephants.

Some fishing boats have huge nets to catch fish.

Fishing

People catch fish to eat or sell. Some use fishing rods, but most fishermen go out to sea with large nets to catch lots of fish at once.

Can you find these things on the maps?

red snappers

butterfly fish

green turtles

scuba diver

seahorses

Tropical reefs

Coral reefs look like sea plants.
In fact, they are made of
thousands of tiny animals, called
corals. The Great Barrier Reef,
near Australia, is the biggest
coral reef in the world.

Coral reefs are found in
warm, shallow seas. Lots of
tropical fish live there too.

Wind surfers use
sails to make their
boards go faster.

Sea sports

Many people enjoy
swimming or splashing
around near the seashore.
Others go surfing on big
waves, or diving under the
water to look at fish.

Shipping ports

Ports are towns by the sea where
ships are loaded and unloaded.
Huge ships carry all kinds of
things, such as food and
fuel, all around the world.

Big cranes
load and
unload ships.

common dolphins   marlin   giant squid   shrimps   blue shark

The world

The world is divided into seven large areas called continents. They are all named in big letters on this map.

The little pictures on this map show some world records.

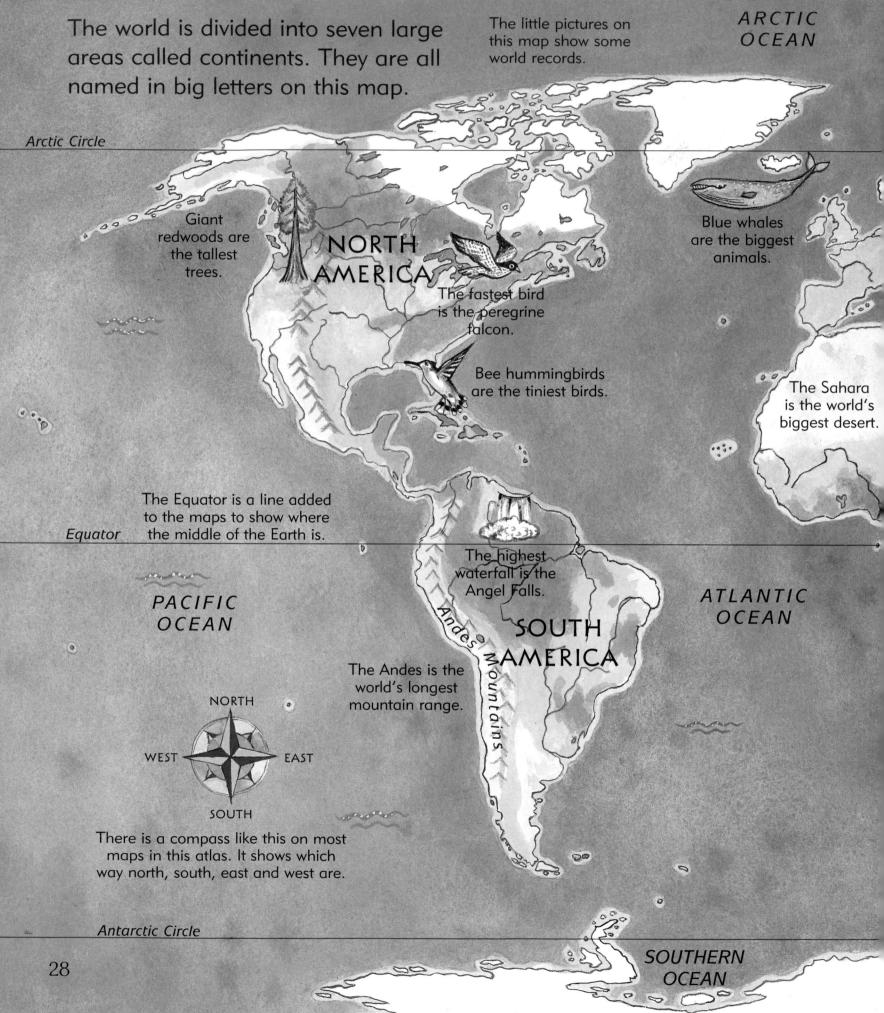

Arctic Circle

Giant redwoods are the tallest trees.

Blue whales are the biggest animals.

NORTH AMERICA

The fastest bird is the peregrine falcon.

Bee hummingbirds are the tiniest birds.

The Sahara is the world's biggest desert.

The Equator is a line added to the maps to show where the middle of the Earth is.

Equator

The highest waterfall is the Angel Falls.

PACIFIC OCEAN

ATLANTIC OCEAN

SOUTH AMERICA

The Andes is the world's longest mountain range.

Andes Mountains

NORTH

WEST   EAST

SOUTH

There is a compass like this on most maps in this atlas. It shows which way north, south, east and west are.

Antarctic Circle

28

SOUTHERN OCEAN

The shading on the maps shows what the land is like in different parts of the world and where there are rivers, lakes, seas and oceans.

ice and snow	deserts	grasslands	forests	mountains	rivers and lakes	seas and oceans

Arctic Circle

ASIA

The Trans-Siberian Express goes along the longest train line.

EUROPE

Mount Everest is the highest mountain.

PACIFIC OCEAN

SAHARA DESERT

The Nile is the longest river.

More people live in China than in any other country.

AFRICA

Whale sharks are the biggest fish.

Cheetahs are the fastest land animals.

Northeast India is the rainiest place in the world.

Rafflesias are the biggest flowers.

Equator

INDIAN OCEAN

Giraffes are the tallest animals.

Uluru (Ayers Rock) is the largest rock in the world.

The biggest bird is the ostrich.

AUSTRALASIA AND OCEANIA

Antarctic Circle

Antarctica is the world's coldest place.

ANTARCTICA

29

North America

ARCTIC OCEAN

GREENLAND

Arctic Circle

Inuit people

Nuuk (Godthåb)

harp seal

cod

ptarmigan

harp seal cub

boy in a kayak

igloo

snowy owl

Canada goose

minke whale

puffins

Paper is made here.

Labrador dog

cranberries

lobster

fishing boat

maple tree

blue jay

Montreal

Ottawa

Arctic terns

wolf

beluga whale

Hudson Bay

cloudberries

beaver

skunk

The Great Lakes

Arctic hare

musk ox

moose

buffalo

icebreaker ship

husky dog

grizzly bear

CANADA

mounted policeman

combine harvester

Missouri River

arctic char

snow goose

muskrat

lumberjack (forester)

skier

ice hockey player

polar bear

Alaska (USA)

caribou

Rocky Mountains

traditional carved pole

Vancouver

Seattle

bald eagle

raccoon

snowmobile

walrus

Anchorage

Gulf of Alaska

Pacific salmon

PACIFIC OCEAN

killer whale

Golden Gate bridge

San Francisco

30

South America

NORTH
EAST
WEST
SOUTH

white shark

Equator

Caribbean Sea

oil rig
■ Caracas
VENEZUELA
Orinoco River
Bogotá ■
COLOMBIA
Coffee is grown here.
Quito ■
EQUADOR

hummingbird
peccary
tapir
fruit bat
iguana
puma
cow
jaguar
condor
arrow poison frog
Angel Falls
scarlet ibis

Georgetown ■
Paramaribo ■
Cayenne ■
rocket base
GUYANA
SURINAME
FRENCH GUIANA

caiman
capybara
sloth
Amazon River
piranha
Madeira River
brazil nuts
spider monkey
llama
Machu Picchu
Andes Mountains
Lima ■
PERU

Amazon Rainforest

armadillo
anaconda
toucan
blue morpho butterfly
orchid
parrot
Tapajos River
BRAZIL

cotton plant
bananas
conga drummer
Sao Francisco River
sugar cane
Gold is mined here.
cocoa beans
Coffee is grown here.
Brasilia Cathedral
Brasilia ■
Tocantins River
Diamonds are mined here.

Guarani people
peanuts
spectacled bear
La Paz ■
BOLIVIA
Sucre ■

girl in a poncho
reed boat on Lake Titicaca
sardines

lobster

shrimps

Equator

32

Rio de Janeiro

sardines

ATLANTIC OCEAN

oil tanker

Sao Paulo

carnival dancers

oranges

surfer

sardines

The world

SOUTH AMERICA

This map shows where South America is.

mackerel

South Georgia

PARAGUAY

Asunción

sheep ranches

URUGUAY

Montevideo

Buenos Aires

tango dancers

albatrosses

Falkland Islands

giant anteater

ARGENTINA

Paraná River

gaucho (cowboy)

rhea

sea lions

chinchilla

Magellan penguin

Cape Horn

Atacama Desert

guanaco

Andes Mountains

sheep

flamingos

CHILE

Santiago

grapes

monkey puzzle tree

rockhopper penguin

pelican

fishing boat

fur seal

southern right whale

mackerel

killer whale

33

Australasia and Oceania

NORTH
WEST · EAST
SOUTH

PACIFIC OCEAN

Northern Mariana Islands

FEDERATED STATES OF MICRONESIA

PALAU

Moorish idol

sea cucumber

Equator

sacred house

crowned pigeon

tree kangaroo

cuscus

dugong

PAPUA NEW GUINEA

Port Moresby

clown fish

pineapple fish

box jellyfish

coral

Great Barrier Reef

harlequin fish

Aboriginal dancer

possum

butterfly fish

spiny anteater

frilled lizard

dingo

koalas

boy diving for pearls

Great Sandy Desert

AUSTRALIA

kangaroos

blue-ringed octopus

bottlenose dolphin

wallaby

thorny devil

Uluru (Ayers Rock)

Opals are mined here.

platypus

Sydney Opera House

grass tree

Great Victoria Desert

Darling River

Sydney

flying doctor

emu

wombat

sheep

parakeet

Canberra

blue-tongued skink

galah

Perth

Melbourne

sea dragon

crayfish

black swan

Tasmania

Tasmanian devil

great white shark

albatrosses

INDIAN OCEAN

MARSHALL
ISLANDS

PACIFIC OCEAN

jumbo jet plane

sea
slug

Hawaiian Islands

girl
wearing
a garland

surfer

fairy terns

angel
fish

cargo ship

NAURU

moray
eel

flying
fish

blue shark

Equator

KIRIBATI

green
turtles

SOLOMON
ISLANDS

parrot
fish

TUVALU

Tokelau

manta
rays

VANUATU

coconut
palms

Wallis and
Futuna

SAMOA American
Samoa

coconuts

fisherman in
a canoe

bananas

rugby
player

TONGA

Niue

sea
horses

tuna

French
Polynesia

FIJI

New
Caledonia

swordfish

Cook
Islands

bananas

Tahiti

snappers

barracudas

giant
squid

The world

kiwi

Maori
dancer

NEW
ZEALAND

Wellington

sperm whale

AUSTRALASIA
AND OCEANIA

This map shows where
Australasia and Oceania are.

sheep

hoki
fish

Asia

Arctic Circle

herring

eider duck

fishing through ice

reindeer

kittiwake

lynx

Ural Mountains

Moscow

Volga River

noctule bat

flying squirrel

man in a fur hat

golden eagle

maize

honeybees

RUSSIA

Astana

saiga antelope

bactrian camel

Blue Mosque

Black Sea

skier

Caspian seal

space agency

wheat

KAZAKHSTAN

Istanbul

Ankara

GEORGIA

Caspian Sea

Aral Sea

Bishkek

jerboa

Gobi Desert

Turkish kebabs

TURKEY

ARMENIA

AZERBAIJAN

UZBEKISTAN

KYRGYZSTAN

Tashkent

Cyprus

SYRIA

TURKMENISTAN

Ashgabat

TAJIKISTAN

snow leopard

Great Wall of China

LEBANON

rug

jackal

ISRAEL

Damascus

AFGHANISTAN

Jerusalem

IRAQ

Tehran

Kabul

Tibetan monks

yak

JORDAN

Baghdad

IRAN

Islamabad

The Himalayas

Mount Everest

KUWAIT

date palms

Afghan hound

New Delhi

NEPAL

BHUTAN

hyena

BAHRAIN

PAKISTAN

Indus River

Kathmandu

oil well

QATAR

Ganges River

Bedouin people

UNITED ARAB EMIRATES

Muscat

Taj Mahal in Agra

BANGLADESH

boy on an elephant

Mecca

Riyadh

OMAN

sitar player

INDIA

Dhaka

water towers

SAUDI ARABIA

girl in a sari

Bengal tiger

Nay Pyi Taw

BURMA

Sana

Arabian horse

Bombay

rickshaw

orchid

YEMEN

Arabian camel

Arabian Sea

Andaman Islands

Bangkok

Red Sea

Socotra

sacred cow

tea plant

floating market

NORTH

Arabian fishing boats

Sri Jayewardenepura Kotte

SRI LANKA

WEST

EAST

Colombo

Kuala Lumpur

SOUTH

oil tanker

MALDIVES

Equator

coral reef

rhinoceros

soldier fish

INDIAN OCEAN

tiger shark

36

snappers

beluga whale

narwhal

polar bears

ringed seal

walrus

Bering Sea

giant kelp forest

lemming

Lena River

snow goose

bearded seal

bowhead whales

brown bear

Siberian tiger

snowmobile

fishing boat

wild mushrooms

Sea of Okhotsk

sea lion

Trans-Siberian Express

sperm whale

pollock

ger (tent)

Kites are made here.

crested puffin

girl in a kimono

PACIFIC OCEAN

Ulan Bator
MONGOLIA

Forbidden City

Vladivostock

NORTH KOREA

bullet train

puffer fish

white-sided dolphin

Beijing

Pyongyang

JAPAN

Seoul

SOUTH KOREA

Tokyo

Terracotta Army

Yellow River

rice plants

crane

sumo wrestler

CHINA

Yangtze River

pagoda

traditional junk (boat)

giant panda

bamboo

Taipei

TAIWAN

octopus

VIETNAM

Hanoi

Hong Kong

South China Sea

dugong

The world

LAOS

Vientiane

THAILAND

Manila

Philippine Sea

ASIA

CAMBODIA

basket boat

THE PHILIPPINES

manta ray

Phnom Penh

This map shows where Asia is.

MALAYSIA

BRUNEI

pineapples

SINGAPORE

Borneo

giant clam

Equator

Sumatra

Celebes

PACIFIC OCEAN

orang-utan

INDONESIA

Jakarta

Java

37

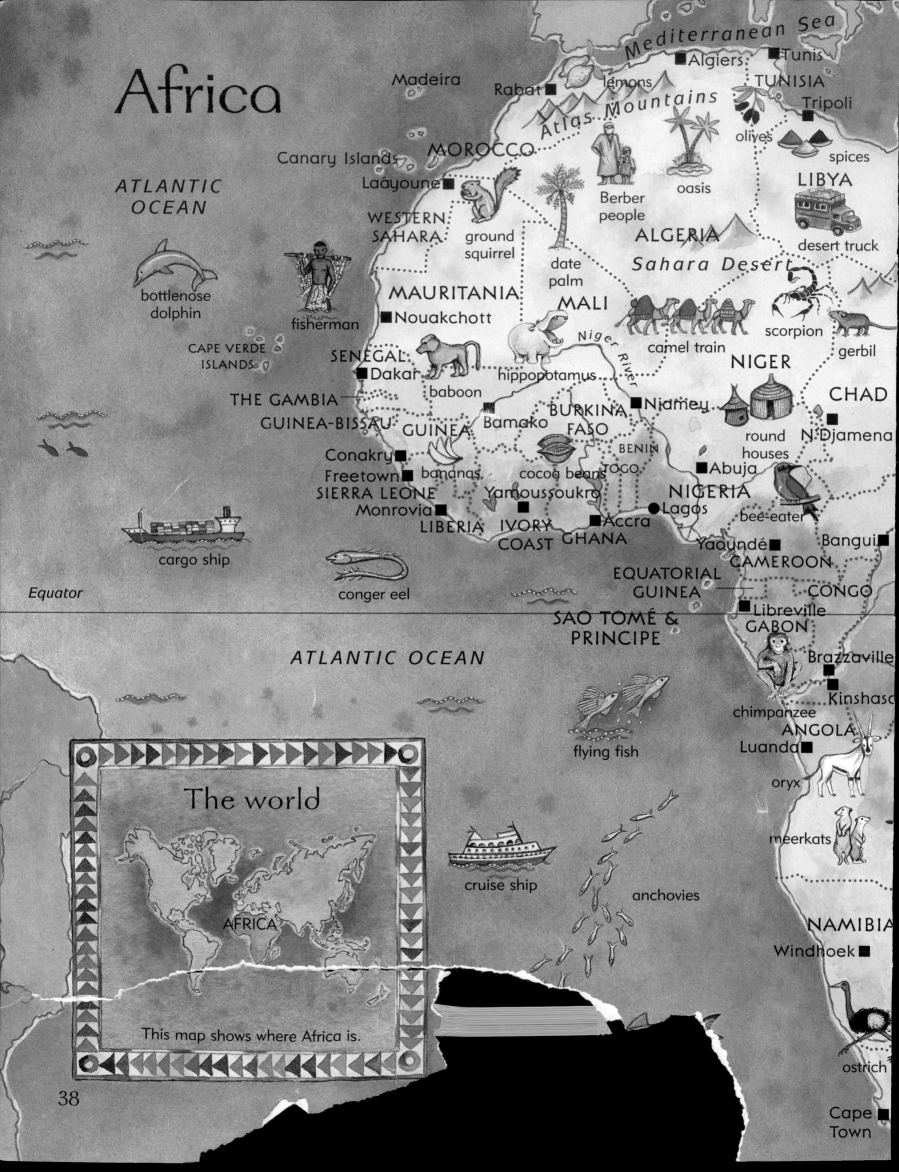

Africa

ATLANTIC OCEAN

Mediterranean Sea

Madeira

Rabat

Algiers
Tunis
TUNISIA
Tripoli

lemons

Atlas Mountains

olives

spices

LIBYA

desert truck

MOROCCO

Canary Islands

Laáyoune

WESTERN SAHARA

ground squirrel

date palm

Berber people

oasis

ALGERIA

Sahara Desert

MAURITANIA

Nouakchott

MALI

camel train

scorpion

gerbil

NIGER

fisherman

CAPE VERDE ISLANDS

bottlenose dolphin

SENEGAL

Dakar

baboon

hippopotamus

Niger River

Niamey

CHAD

N'Djamena

round houses

THE GAMBIA

GUINEA-BISSAU

GUINEA

Bamako

BURKINA FASO

BENIN

Conakry

Freetown

bananas

cocoa beans

TOGO

Abuja

NIGERIA

Lagos

bee-eater

SIERRA LEONE

Yamoussoukro

Monrovia

Accra

LIBERIA

IVORY COAST

GHANA

Yaoundé

Bangui

CAMEROON

cargo ship

conger eel

EQUATORIAL GUINEA

CONGO

Equator

SAO TOMÉ & PRINCIPE

Libreville

GABON

ATLANTIC OCEAN

Brazzaville

Kinshasa

chimpanzee

flying fish

ANGOLA

Luanda

The world

oryx

AFRICA

cruise ship

anchovies

meerkats

NAMIBIA

Windhoek

This map shows where Africa is.

ostrich

38

Cape Town

Africa

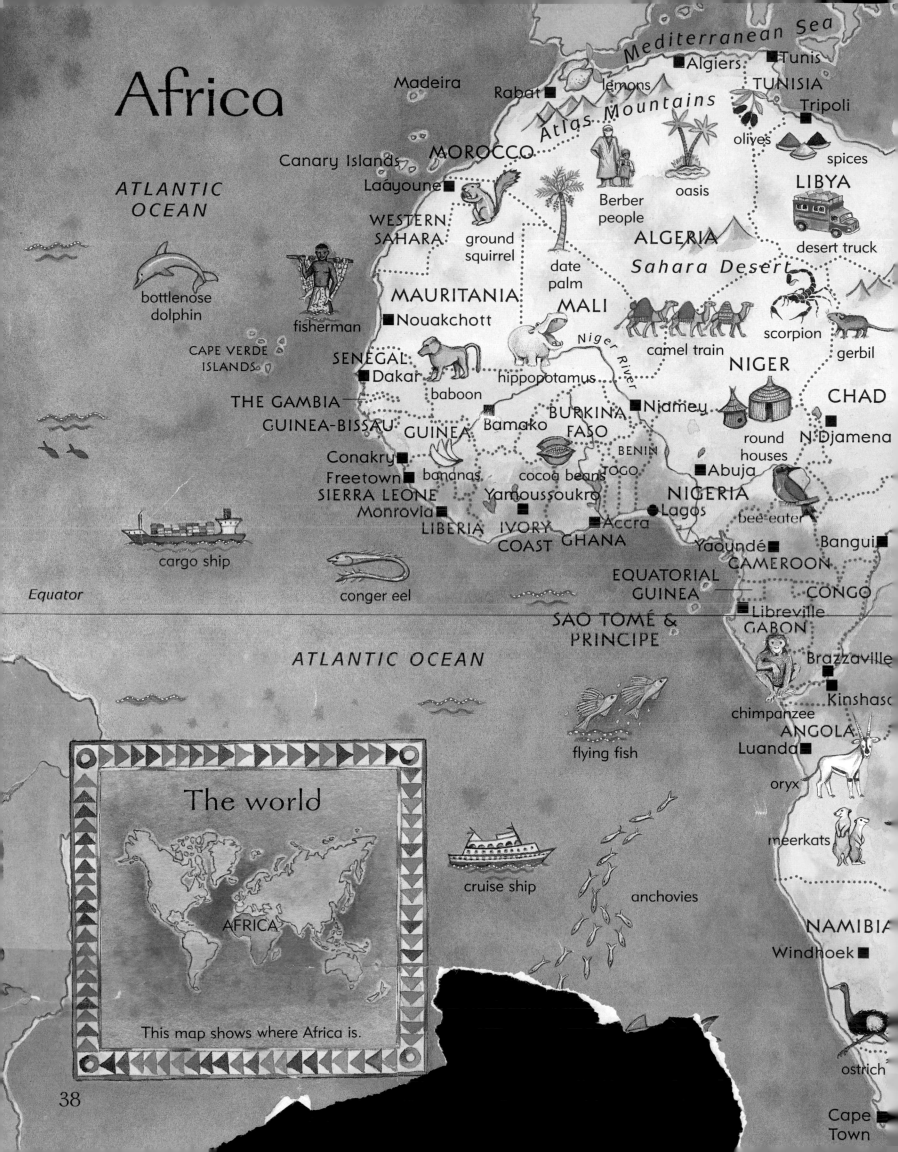

Mediterranean Sea

Algiers ■   ■ Tunis
Rabat ■   lemons   TUNISIA
Madeira   Atlas Mountains   Tripoli ■
MOROCCO   olives   spices
Canary Islands   Berber   oasis   LIBYA
Laáyoune ■   people
ATLANTIC   ground   ALGERIA   desert truck
OCEAN   WESTERN   squirrel
SAHARA   date   Sahara Desert
palm
bottlenose   MAURITANIA   MALI   scorpion
dolphin   Nouakchott ■   camel train   NIGER   gerbil
fisherman   Niger River
CAPE VERDE   hippopotamus   CHAD
ISLANDS   SENEGAL   Niamey ■   N'Djamena ■
Dakar ■   baboon   BURKINA
THE GAMBIA   Bamako ■   FASO   round
GUINEA-BISSAU   GUINEA   BENIN   houses   Abuja ■
Conakry ■   bananas   cocoa beans   TOGO
Freetown ■   Yamoussoukro ■   NIGERIA   bee-eater
SIERRA LEONE   Accra   Lagos ●
Monrovia ■   IVORY   Yaoundé ■   Bangui
cargo ship   LIBERIA   COAST   GHANA   CAMEROON
Equator   EQUATORIAL   CONGO
conger eel   GUINEA   Libreville ■
SAO TOMÉ &   GABON
PRINCIPE   Brazzaville ■
ATLANTIC OCEAN   chimpanzee   Kinshasa ■
ANGOLA
flying fish   Luanda ■
oryx

meerkats

cruise ship   anchovies   NAMIBIA

Windhoek ■

The world

AFRICA

This map shows where Africa is.

ostrich

Cape
Town

38

beluga whale

narwhal

polar bears

ringed seal

walrus

Bering Sea

giant kelp forest

bowhead whales

lemming

Lena River

snow goose

snowmobile

bearded seal

brown bear

Siberian tiger

Sea of Okhotsk

fishing boat

wild mushrooms

Trans-Siberian Express

sea lion

sperm whale

pollock

ger (tent)

Kites are made here.

crested puffin

girl in a kimono

PACIFIC OCEAN

■ Ulan Bator

MONGOLIA

Forbidden City

Vladivostock

NORTH KOREA

bullet train

puffer fish

white-sided dolphin

Beijing ■

■ Pyongyang

JAPAN

Terracotta Army

Yellow River

Seoul

SOUTH KOREA

■ Tokyo

rice plants

CHINA

Yangtze River

crane

sumo wrestler

The world

giant panda

bamboo

pagoda

traditional junk (boat)

■ Taipei

TAIWAN

VIETNAM

■ Hanoi

Hong Kong

South China Sea

dugong

octopus

ASIA

LAOS

Vientiane

THAILAND

Manila

Philippine Sea

CAMBODIA

■

basket boat

THE PHILIPPINES

manta ray

This map shows where Asia is.

Phnom Penh

MALAYSIA

BRUNEI

pineapples

SINGAPORE

Borneo

giant clam

Celebes

Equator

Sumatra

orang-utan

rubber trees

New

INDON

■ Jakarta

Java

temple

37

Saami people

reindeer

puffins

flounder

fishing through ice

Arctic hare

capercaillie

SWEDEN

wolverine

wild mushrooms

sparrow hawk

Ural owl

Ural Mountains

Siberian chipmunk

moose

FINLAND

lynx

sable

ballet dancers

wheat

Baltic Sea

Paper is made here.

Helsinki ■

Winter Palace in St. Petersburg

beaver

RUSSIA

gymnast

■ Stockholm   Tallinn ■

ESTONIA

■ Moscow

sprats

LATVIA

cow   Riga ■

red fox

St. Basil's Cathedral

maize

wild horses

LITHUANIA

Volga River

Vilnius ■

potatoes

■ Moscow

black stork

Ships are made here.

Minsk ■

BELARUS

wild boar

Russian dolls

POLAND

■ Warsaw

deer

European bison

brown bear

chamois

Kiev ■

Dnieper River

Cossack dancer

Don River

balalaika player

Caspian Sea

ECH BLIC

SLOVAKIA

UKRAINE

na

atislava

Carpathian Mountains

MOLDOVA

Chisinau

sunflowers

castle

ROMANIA

space telescope

The world

BOSNIA & HERZEGOVINA

Belgrade ■

SERBIA

■ Bucharest

Danube River

sturgeon

Sarajevo

MONTENEGRO   KOSOVO

BULGARIA

Black Sea

EUROPE

ortress in brovnik

Pristina ■

Sofia ■

grapes

Tirana ■

MACEDONIA

■ Istanbul

ALBANIA

TURKEY

olives

GREECE

This map shows where Europe is.

olives

■ Athens

Parthenon

Crete   olives   fishing boat

41

The Arctic

Bering Sea

Sea of Okhotsk

Gulf of Alaska

fishing boat

volcanoes

snowmobile

walrus

bearded seal

Chukchi tent

Alaska (USA)

husky racer

moose

Chukchi Sea

Wrangel Island

purple heron

Siberian tiger

wolf

Beaufort Sea

Arctic loon

RUSSIA

CANADA

polar bear

New Siberia Islands

snowy owl

salmon

ARCTIC OCEAN

Laptev Sea

Canada goose

Arctic fox

Arctic terns

helicopter

narwhal

lynx

stoat

Arctic hare

Severnaya Zemlya

lemming

Ellesmere Island

ringed seal

North Pole

Kara Sea

Baffin Island

explorer

Franz Josef Land

Arctic poppies

Arctic chars

caribou

polar bear

Novaya Zemlya

GREENLAND

harp seal

satellite station

Barents Sea

boy in a kayak

Nuuk (Godthab)

musk ox

minke whale

Arctic Circle

ptarmigan

puffins

cod

Reykjavik

ICELAND

ATLANTIC OCEAN

ferry

fishing boat

The world

THE ARCTIC

ANTARCTICA

The Arctic and Antarctica are on opposite sides of the world.

Antarctica

South Georgia

ATLANTIC OCEAN

SOUTHERN OCEAN

Africa is this way.

sea bass

blue whale

krill

snail fish

wandering albatrosses

cruise ship

Weddell Sea

robot submarine

macaroni penguin

scientist with a weather balloon

Adélie penguins

INDIAN OCEAN

British science station

Ronne Ice Shelf

ANTARCTICA

fur seal

leopard seal

South America is this way.

Antarctic Peninsula

Weddell seal

South Pole

American science station

rockhopper penguin

chinstrap penguin

caterpillar truck

brittle star

Antarctic Circle

gentoo penguins

snowmobile

Transantarctic Mountains

ski plane

elephant seal

Ross Ice Shelf

Australian science station

krill

emperor penguins

Ross Sea

soft coral

king penguin

blue-eyed shag

French science station

giant petrels

ice fish

krill

porbeagle shark

SOUTHERN OCEAN

PACIFIC OCEAN

Australia is this way.

Arctic terns

killer whale

43

A trip around the world

Are you ready for a trip around the world?
Look back through this book and try this
fun quiz to find out. The answers
are all on page 48.

Packing your bags

You'll need to pack
carefully for your trip.
Can you match
these things to the
places where
you'll need them?

1. Climbing boots
2. A warm coat
3. A water bottle
4. A diving suit

a. The Arctic
b. Mount Everest
c. The Atacama Desert
d. The Great Barrier Reef

Things to see

1. Would you see
penguins in the Arctic or
in Antarctica?

2. In which town in Italy
would you see canals
instead of roads?

3. Which is the only
country where you can
see koalas and
kangaroos in the wild?

4. Which city in Brazil
would you visit to see
people dressed up for
a carnival?

44

Country shapes

Here are the shapes of some of the countries you might visit. Can you recognize them from the maps?

4.

1.

2.

3.

Blue clues

Can you find and name all of these things with "blue" in their names?

1. A butterfly that lives in the Amazon rainforest.

2. An octopus that swims near Australia.

3. An Australian lizard with an unusual tongue.

4. A North American bird.

People to meet

In which countries would you expect to meet these people?

1. Hopi dancer
2. Girl in a kimono
3. Reggae singer
4. Zulu dancer

Index of places

Index of things

Answers

Things to spot

Countries and cities
Big Ben, 40
Parthenon, 41
St. Basil's Cathedral, 41
Forbidden City, 37
Eiffel Tower, 40
Blue Mosque, 36
Winter Palace in St. Petersburg, 41
Leaning Tower of Pisa, 40
Sydney Opera House, 34
Statue of Liberty, 31

People
Guarani people, 32
Zulu dancer, 39
sitar player, 36
rugby player, 35
highland piper, 40
conga drummer, 32
Tibetan monks, 36
Hopi dancer, 31
girl in a poncho, 32
American football player, 31

Getting around
basket boat, 37
desert truck, 38
traditional junk (boat), 37
Trans-Siberian Express, 29, 37
helicopter, 42

Ice and snow
ice fish, 43
humpback whale, 40
American science station, 43
Arctic fox, 42
Saami people, 41

Deserts
fennec fox, 39
jerboa, 36
blue-tongued skink, 34
scorpion, 38
rattlesnake, 31

Grasslands
kangaroos, 34
guanaco, 33
buffalo, 30
giraffe, 39
meerkats, 38

lion, 39
giant anteater, 33
African elephant, 39
oryx, 38
rhea, 33

Forests
blue morpho butterfly, 32
armadillo, 32
red fox, 41
raccoon, 30
anaconda, 32
grizzly bear, 30
wild mushrooms, 37
lumberjack (forester), 30
chimpanzee, 38
toucan, 32

Mountains
bald eagle, 30
Mount Everest, 29, 36
yak, 36
chamois, 41
Ural owl, 41

Rivers and lakes
capybara, 32
piranha, 32

Caspian seal, 36
hippopotamus, 38
felucca boat, 39

Seas and oceans
red snappers, 31
butterfly fish, 34
green turtles, 35
scuba diver, 31
seahorses, 35
common dolphins, 31
marlin, 31
giant squid, 35
shrimps, 32
blue shark, 35

A trip around the world

Packing your bags
1. b. You'll need climbing boots on Mount Everest.
2. a. A warm coat will keep out the cold in the Arctic.
3. c. The Atacama Desert is the driest place on Earth, so you'll need a water bottle.

4. d. You'll need a diving suit to dive down to the Great Barrier Reef.

Places to see
1. Antarctica
2. Venice
3. Australia
4. Rio de Janeiro

Country shapes
1. New Zealand
2. Mexico
3. Australia
4. Italy

Blue clues
1. Blue morpho butterfly
2. Blue-ringed octopus
3. Blue-tongued skink
4. Blue jay

People to meet
1. USA
2. Japan
3. Jamaica
4. South Africa

Managing editor: Gillian Doherty   Managing designer: Russell Punter
The publishers are grateful to the following organizations and individuals for their permission to reproduce material.
p6 This image is an extract from the Millennium Map™ which is © getmapping.com plc; **p7** ©Tom Van Sant, Geosphere Project/Planetary Visions/Science Photo Library